Under my Feet

Written by Malaika Rose Stanley

Illustrated by Geraldine Rodriguez

Published by Pearson Education Limited, 80 Strand, London, WC2R 0RL.

www.pearsonschools.co.uk

Text © Pearson Education Limited 2017

Designed by Andrew Magee Design
Original illustrations © Pearson Education Limited
Illustrated by Geraldine Rodriguez

First published 2017

2024
10
British Library Cataloguing in Publication Data
A catalogue record for this book is available from the British Library

ISBN 978 0 435 16481 2

Copyright notice
All rights reserved. No part of this publication may be reproduced in any form or by any means (including photocopying or storing it in any medium by electronic means and whether or not transiently or incidentally to some other use of this publication) without the written permission of the copyright owner, except in accordance with the provisions of the Copyright, Designs and Patents Act 1988 or under the terms of a licence issued by the Copyright Licensing Agency, Barnards Inn, 86 Fetter Lane, London, EC4A 1EN (www.cla.co.uk). Applications for the copyright owner's written permission should be addressed to the publisher.

Printed in the UK by Ashford Colour Press.

Under my feet, beneath the street,
there are basements for snow boots, buggies and bikes,
and rickety chairs that nobody likes.
Deep down, under the ground.

Under my feet, beneath the street,
there are cellars and store rooms, all dusty and cold,
safe boxes for jewels and bank vaults for gold.
Deep down, under the ground.

Under my feet, beneath the street,
there are internet cables and wires for phones,
snail shell fossils and dinosaur bones.
Deep down, under the ground.

Under my feet, beneath the street,
there are ticket machines and train operators,
"Watch your step!" stairs and "Stand still!" escalators.
Deep down, under the ground.

Under my feet, beneath the street,
there's a ramp for a digger, a track for a truck,
excavating and carrying out muck.
Deep down, under the ground.

Under my feet, beneath the street,
there are walkways for people under roadways for cars,
where buskers sing songs and play on guitars.
Deep down, under the ground.

Under my feet, beneath the street,
there are long, twisty pipelines for gas and for oil,
and wiggly worms that squirm through the soil.
Deep down, under the ground.

Under my feet, beneath the street,
there are footings for buildings and roots of huge trees,
old buried treasure, lost coins and keys.
Deep down, under the ground.

Under my feet, beneath the street,
there are bunkers and shelters built during the war
for top-secret planners, code crackers and more.
Deep down, under the ground.

Under my feet, beneath the street,
there are seeds and bulbs shooting up to the sun,
and all around me, new life has begun.
Deep down, under the ground.